INSIDE A
POWERBOAT

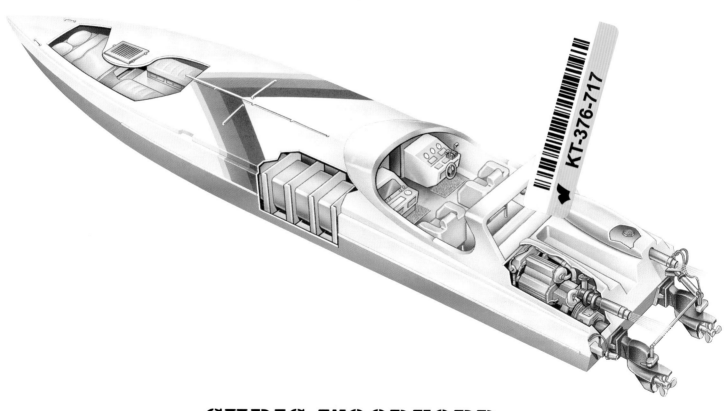

CHRIS WOODFORD

angus

This edition published in 2004
by Angus Books Ltd
12 Ravensbury Terrace
London SW18 4RL

ISBN 1-904594-53-0

FOR BROWN PARTWORKS
Project editor: Tom Jackson
Consultant: Dr. Donald R. Franceschetti
Designer: Sarah Williams
Illustrators: Roger Courthold (main artwork), Mark Walker
Managing editor: Anne O'Daly
Picture researcher: Sean Hannaway

Production by Omnipress,
Eastbourne, UK
Printed and bound in Dubai

Contents

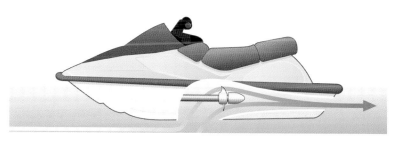

Powerboats in the past

Powerboats have become faster throughout history. Once sailboats were the fastest things on water. Now powerful engines make powerboats travel as fast as cars.

Early Native Americans thought their bark canoes were high-speed boats, even though they were paddled by people. The ancient Egyptians thought the same about their sailboats and the Greeks rowed in triremes, which were the fastest boats of their time. Today's high-speed boats are driven by engines and travel many times faster.

The age of steam

Modern high-speed boats were born when people put engines in boats and used fuels to drive them. The first fuel used was coal. It was burned to produce steam in a boiler

rather like a huge kettle. The steam pushed a piston up and down and it turned a propeller that pushed the boat forward. The first steamboat was made in 1801 by Scottish engineer William Symington (1763–1831). A better design was used by English engineer

Turbinia was the fastest boat of its time. Its engine design was used to power huge steamships that crossed the world's oceans.

The jet-powered *Bluebird* broke the world record in 1964. In 1967 the *Bluebird* crashed while travelling at 300 mph (480km/h), killing its driver.

A modern replica of an ancient Greek trireme. Triremes had 170 oars in three rows and could travel at 10 mph (16km/h) for short distances.

Sir Charles Parsons (1854–1931) in his yacht *Turbinia* in 1887. Instead of using a piston, the steam turned a kind of windmill called a turbine. It was faster and used less fuel.

Better, further, faster

Coal took up too much space, and better engines were soon developed. German engineer Gottlieb Daimler (1834–1900) invented the petrol engine used in cars today and powered a boat with one in 1887. In 1906 Italian engineer Enrico Forlanini (1848–1930) made the first hydrofoil.

War and peace

High-speed boats had many uses. The U.S. Navy found motorboats, such as their small Patrol Torpedo (PT) boat, very effective in World War II (1939–1945). Boating has also become a popular leisure activity and a sport. The first international powerboat competition was held on the Hudson River in 1904 and people were soon setting speed records in motorboats. In 1964 Englishman Donald Campbell (1921–1967) set a water-speed record of 276 mph (444km/h) in *Bluebird*, but he died trying to go even faster. Today's fastest boat, *Spirit of Australia*, set a record of 318 mph (511km/h) in 1978.

FACT FILE

◯ The fastest man on water is Australian Ken Warby (1940–). His jet boat, *Spirit of Australia*, broke the record using less than full power.

◯ Donald Campbell's father, Malcolm, also held the water-speed record. Both men also broke the land-speed record as well.

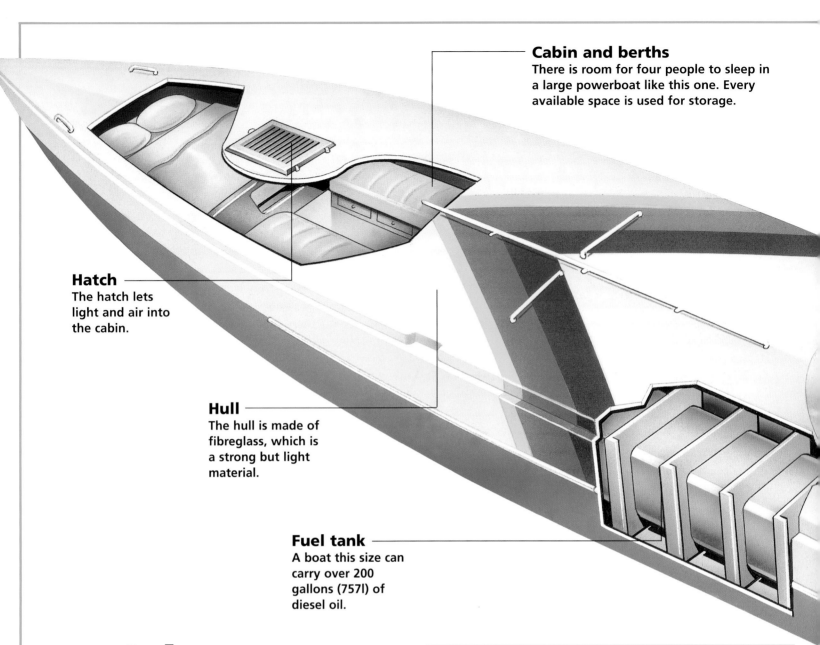

Cabin and berths
There is room for four people to sleep in a large powerboat like this one. Every available space is used for storage.

Hatch
The hatch lets light and air into the cabin.

Hull
The hull is made of fibreglass, which is a strong but light material.

Fuel tank
A boat this size can carry over 200 gallons (757l) of diesel oil.

Inside a powerboat

Powerboats are designed to cut through the water, so they all have the same pointed shape. However, most boats are painted with bright, colourful patterns and so few of them look too much alike. Boats like this are mainly driven out at sea because they go far too fast for rivers and lakes.

FACT FILE

○ On a boat the words *port* and *starboard* are used instead of *left* and *right*. The front end of a boat is called the bow. The back is called the stern.

○ Powerboats are not cheap! Boats like the one above would cost about $250,000, and many cost a lot more.

○ Most fast leisure boats only need about 4 ft (1.2m) of water to float in safely. However, there is not much room on board. The cabin's ceiling is only about 5 ft (1.5m) high, so few people can stand up straight.

Offshore powerboat

Instrument panel
Information about the engines is displayed on this panel in front of the driver.

Controls
The boat's speed is controlled by the throttle levers, and the driver steers using the wheel.

Airfoil
This structure acts like an upside-down wing. It pushes the boat back into the water and keeps it from flipping over at high speed.

Air intake
The air used to burn the engine fuel is sucked in through this opening. It is covered to stop too much water getting in.

Hydraulic steering
Hydraulic pistons turn the outdrives to steer the boat. The outdrives are linked together, so they always turn by the same amount.

Engine
Large powerboats like this one have two engines, one on either side. These engines are powered by diesel oil.

Gearbox
The speed of the propellers is controlled by this device.

Exhaust outlet
Waste gases and the water used to cool the engine are pushed out of the engine through here.

Outdrive
Power from the engine goes to the propeller through the outdrive.

Propeller
The propellers spin around and push the boat along.

7

Building fast boats

High-speed boats have to be very tough. Coast Guard boats have to stay afloat in very rough water, and racing powerboats have to protect the driver during a crash. The way boats are put together is very important.

Engineers test the stability of a model boat in a wave tank. Waves of different sizes are sent up and down the tank to make the model move as if it were a full-sized boat at sea.

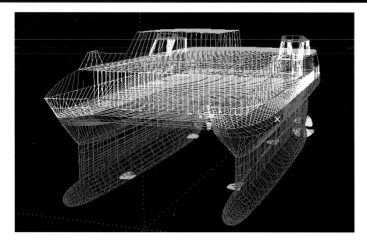
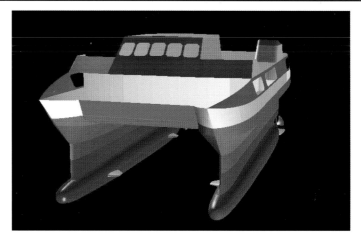

A computer can create a three-dimensional image of a new boat design. Boatbuilders can see the internal structure of the hull (left) as well as what the outside would look like (right).

Most boats, from the smallest rowboat to the biggest oil tanker, are now designed using a computer. Different shaped hulls (the part of a boat that touches the water) are tried by the computer to test their stability (how steady the boat will be) and manoeuvrability (how well it steers) and to work out how much it will cost to make.

Boatbuilding materials

Many different materials are used to make boats. Wood, once the main boatbuilding material, has been replaced by light metals, such as aluminium, tough plastic, such as fibreglass and a very strong material called Kevlar. Inflatable boats are built from a rubbery material called neoprene, which is also used to make wetsuits. Neoprene is very strong and unlike other rubber, it is not damaged by sunlight and oil. Lifeboats often have a layer of polystyrene in the hull to keep them afloat even when they are damaged.

Building a powerboat

Just like jelly, plastic powerboats are made from a mould. Because one mould is used to make hundreds of boats, it must be absolutely perfect, or boats made in it may break. Inside the mould the hull is built up in layers by sticking pieces of soft fibreglass together with a liquid adhesive called resin. The fibreglass is made hard either using chemicals or by putting the boat in an oven (called a kiln).

WHAT FLOATS?

1 Draw this shape onto a piece of newspaper and fold it into a box, clipping it shut with paperclips. How long does it float?

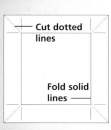

Cut dotted lines

Fold solid lines

2 Try the same thing with paper towel, wax paper, magazine pages and different types of cardboard. Which one floats longest?

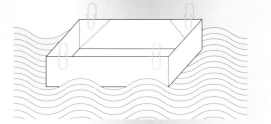

9

Engine power

Once boats were powered by people pulling oars through the water or by the force of the wind pushing against sails. But to travel any distance in any type of weather, a boat needs an engine.

Boat engines are usually petrol- or diesel-powered. Petrol engines cost less and are smaller and lighter than diesel engines. But petrol fumes can collect in the bottom of boats and explode, so petrol engines are also more dangerous. The big diesel engines used

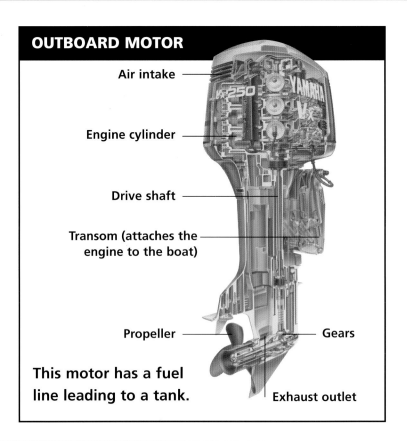

OUTBOARD MOTOR

Air intake

Engine cylinder

Drive shaft

Transom (attaches the engine to the boat)

Propeller

Gears

This motor has a fuel line leading to a tank.

Exhaust outlet

MAKE A BOAT ENGINE

You will need a juice carton, a cork, two pencils, rubber bands and some plastic.

1 Attach two pencils to the empty juice carton with rubber bands.

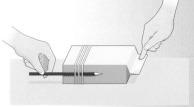

2 Ask an adult to cut four grooves along the side of the cork.

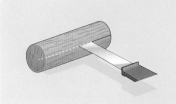

3 Cut plastic paddles as wide as the cork and stick them in two of the grooves.

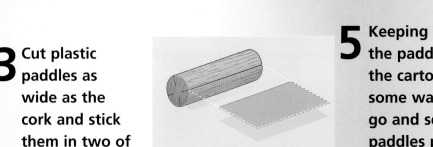

4 Using another rubber band, attach the cork to the end of the pencils. Make sure the band goes along the two grooves. Twist the cork around until the rubber band is tightly wound.

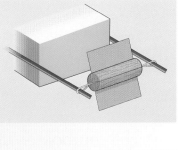

5 Keeping hold of the paddles, put the carton in some water. Let go and see the paddles push the carton along!

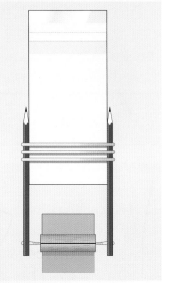

Large boats have their engines inside the hull. Inboard engines are very heavy, and they are kept below the water line to keep the boat stable. The fuel tank is also at the bottom of the boat.

Deck

Cabin

Engine

Gearbox

Exhaust pipe

Fuel tank

Water line

Propeller

Driveshaft

in trucks are more powerful than the small petrol engines used in cars. The same goes for boats. Big boats like deep-sea powerboats use tough diesel engines and small pleasure boats use smaller petrol engines.

In and out

Boat engines come in two types called inboard and outboard. Inboard engines fit completely inside the boat but take up a lot of room. That is why another type of engine was invented for smaller boats. It is called an outboard motor and it is very light and compact. It hangs over the back of the boat, takes up only little space inside and allows more room for people and cargo on board.

An inboard engine is connected to a driveshaft, which makes propellers spin around and push the boat forward, by a system of gears (toothed wheels). The gears can make the driveshaft turn less often than the engine does. This is more efficient and allows the driver to slow and even stop the

propeller without stopping the engine. The engine, gears, driveshaft and sometimes the fuel tank of an outboard motor are all packed together in one unit. Outboards can easily be taken off the boat when they are not needed.

This power cruiser has a large inboard engine. Inboard engines are more powerful than outboard motors and all big boats have them.

Inside the cockpit

Because they travel so quickly, high-speed boats must be easy to steer and control. This is usually done in the part of the powerboat known as the cockpit, where the driver sits.

Small boats with outboard motors have no cockpit. They are steered by swivelling the entire motor, which makes the propeller push the boat in a different direction. Bigger boats, such as those used by the U.K. Coast Guard, have a cockpit like the one on a big ship. Large cockpits like this are known as the bridge and have a steering wheel and a dashboard with instruments like a speedometer and a fuel gauge. The cockpit

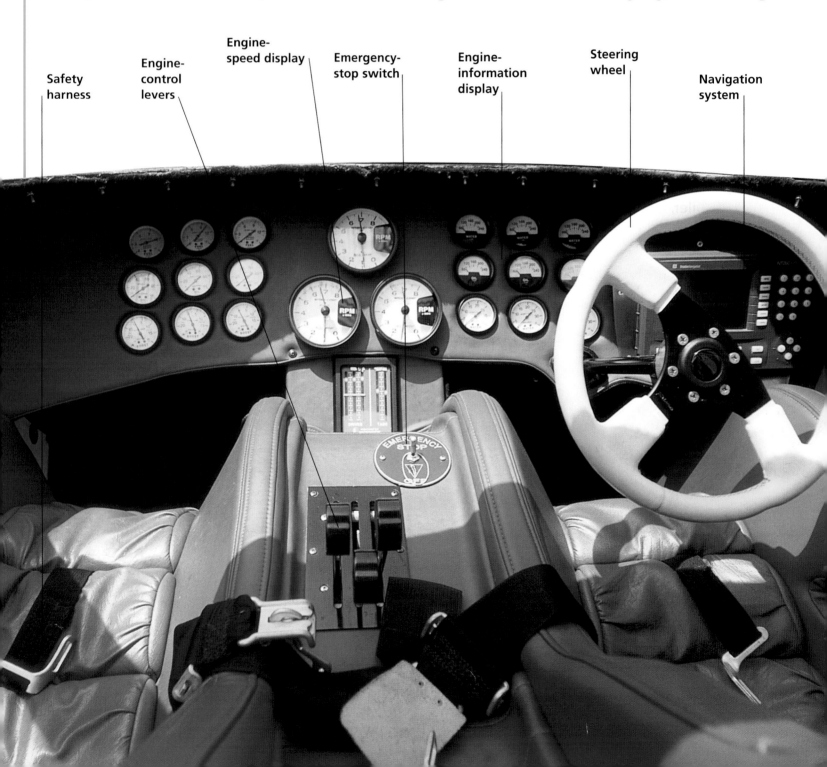

Safety harness

Engine-control levers

Engine-speed display

Emergency-stop switch

Engine-information display

Steering wheel

Navigation system

HOW TO STEER A BOAT

With the rudder straight, the current of water pushes the boat straight forward.

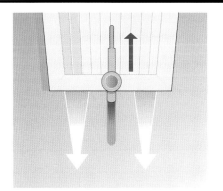

When the rudder handle is moved to the left, the current pushes on the rudder. This turns the boat to the right.

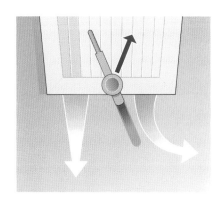

In the same way, when the handle, or tiller, is moved to the right, the boat is forced over to the left.

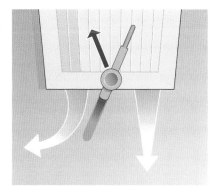

Steering with an outboard engine is similar to this. By moving the engine, the propeller can push the boat in any direction.

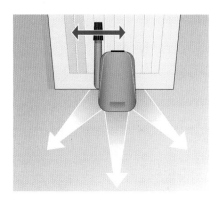

Left: The cockpit of a high-speed powerboat. The cockpit looks a bit like the front seats of a fast car, but there are no foot pedals. The engines are controlled using the levers in the centre.

also contains devices to help the boat find its way (navigate), including a compass, radar and radio. Racing boats have smaller cockpits, but they contain the same sort of things.

Steering a boat

Fast boats have steering wheels, but they are not steered like cars. The engine and the steering equipment are at the back of a boat, and this makes it move in a different way.

A boat's propeller pushes out a current of water. This current is forced against a swivelling blade called a rudder. The rudder deflects the current in different directions, and it is this that turns the boat. But there are some odd effects. The current is greater when the propeller turns faster, so the rudder turns the boat more at high speed than at low speed. It can be hard to steer a boat at low speed and almost impossible to steer in reverse. Because boats do not have brakes, they can only be stopped by putting the engine into reverse.

Some big boats steer using outdrives. They are half like an outboard and half like an inboard engine. An outdrive is a movable casing around the propeller. The power that turns the propeller comes from the engine onboard the boat, but the whole outdrive can turn to steer the boat. This way outdrives steer in the same way as outboard motors.

Why do boats float?

Science is very important in boatbuilding because it explains how forces act on objects in water. This helps people make boats that float well and move swiftly through the waves.

Greek mathematician Archimedes was the first person to explain why boats float on water. Getting into his bathtub, over two thousand years ago, he saw water spill over the top and realized that the amount of water spilled (or displaced) was the same as the volume of his own body.

An object floats if its total weight is less than the weight of water it pushes aside when it sits in the water. Floating is caused by an upward force on the boat called buoyancy. The more weight a boat carries, the lower it sits in the water.

HULL SHAPES

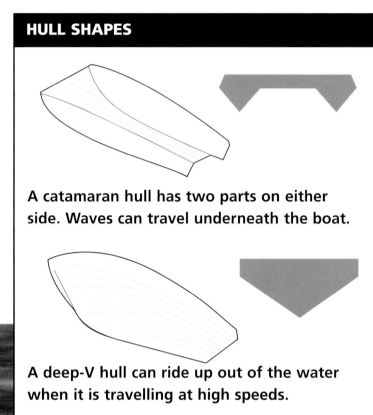

A catamaran hull has two parts on either side. Waves can travel underneath the boat.

A deep-V hull can ride up out of the water when it is travelling at high speeds.

Hull shape

Keeping a boat afloat means spreading its weight out evenly so it does not sink at one end. Any heavy objects must also be kept low down to keep the boat from tipping over (capsizing). That is why the engine is always at the bottom of a boat's hull.

The shape of a hull affects a boat's stability (steadiness) and speed. Boats that sit low in the water are slowed by the waves as they move through them. Fast powerboats have a deep-V-shaped hull at the front end (bow). At high speeds the bow rises above the waves and drags in the water much less, so the boat goes faster. This is known as planing. There are different ways of shaping a hull to increase planing. Catamarans have two small hulls on each side that hold the rest of the boat out of the water. Hydrofoil boats have underwater wings that lift the hull out of the water completely at high speeds.

TESTING DRAG

You will need some plasticine, string, a small weight and a watertight plastic box.

1 Tie a ball of plasticine to a weight, maybe a small piece of wood, that is about the same weight as the ball.

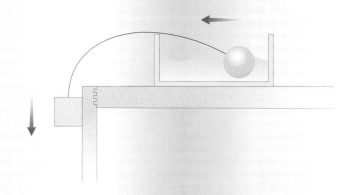

2 Put the ball at one end of the box. Fill the box with water until the ball is almost covered. Drop the weight. How long does it take for the the ball to move to the other end of the box?

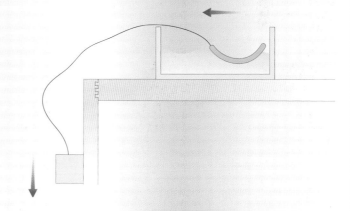

3 Now make the ball into a flattened boat shape that floats on the water. Repeat the test. The boat shape travels faster because it planes over the water.

Left: A powerboat with a deep-V hull planes across the surface of the water.

Forward thrust

Propellers make a boat move in the water. Like the propeller on an aeroplane, a boat's propeller provides a thrust force that pushes the boat forwards.

If you stand on a skateboard and kick back with your foot, the skateboard and your body moves forward down the road. This was explained by English mathematician Sir Isaac Newton's (1642–1727) laws of physics. Newton's laws explain that whenever one force pushes on an object (the force of your kick), another equal force is created that pushes the object in the opposite direction (the force that pushes you down the road).

A park ranger drives his airboat across a lake in Florida. This boat does not have a propeller under the water, so it can cross very shallow water.

A propeller works in this way too. As the propeller's blades turn, they push water away from the boat and this moves the boat in the other direction. To work properly, propellers need to be fully submerged (completely underwater). They can help steer a boat by

Personal watercraft, such as jet-skis and sea-doos, are powered by jets of water.

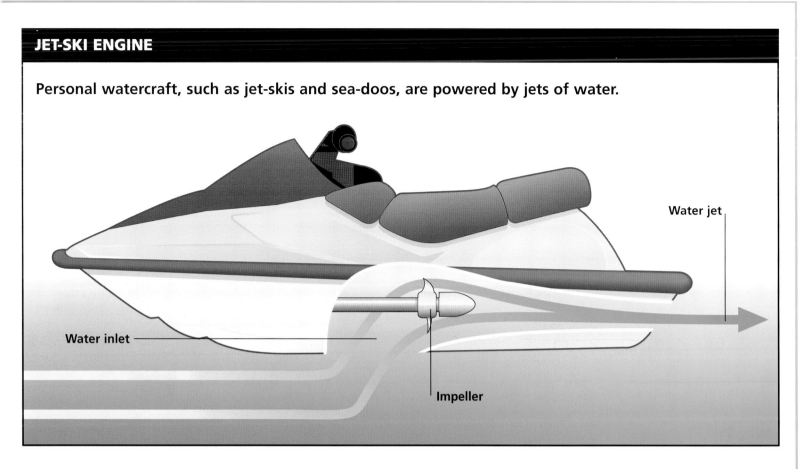

Water jet

Water inlet

Impeller

pushing water directly onto the rudder or by swivelling around themselves and changing the direction of the force.

Jet drives

Not all boats use rotating blades to push them along. In shallow rocky waters the blades of a propeller could break off and leave the boat stranded. Airboats with huge air propellers are used instead in these areas.

Where people are swimming, the blades could cause a nasty injury. A better type of propeller in these conditions is the jet drive. It uses a powerful impeller (a propeller that pulls rather than pushes) to suck water into the front of the boat and push it out in a high-speed jet at the back. The boat can be steered by swivelling the jet or by changing the force of two separate jets. Jet drives are used on personal watercraft, such as jet-skis, and on very fast boats called jetfoils.

A propeller can be seen as a racing boat is lifted out of the water.

High-speed travel

Ferries are boats that carry a lot of people and cargo back and forth between two points. Many are very large and can only travel slowly. However, some ferries can carry their passengers at very high speeds.

Ferries need to carry as many people as possible, so they are generally big boats that cannot travel very fast. However, some modern ferries use the latest engines and boatbuilding technology to carry many passengers, cars and trucks at high speed. High-speed ferries make more money for the ferry company because they can make more trips in a day than slower ones.

Aeroplanes of the sea

Hydrofoils look very much like normal boats except that they have wings mounted on legs beneath the hull. With an aeroplane, air moves faster over the top surface of the wings than the bottom surface. This reduces the pressure above the wing and produces a force called lift that holds the aeroplane in the sky. The same

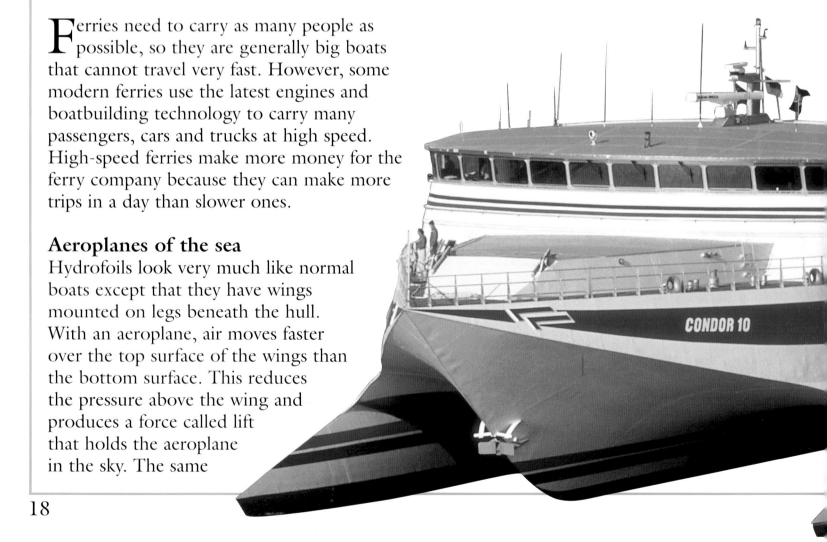

Left: This hydrofoil ferry can carry passengers at high speed. On normal ferries the journey could take hours longer.

thing happens in a hydrofoil. At low speeds the hull drags in the water like any other boat. At higher speeds the underwater wings produce so much lift that the entire hull can rise up out of the water. Riding above the waves, the hull is not slowed down by the water and the boat can move much faster.

Jetfoils are a special type of hydrofoil driven by a jet of water rather than a propeller. In the biggest jetfoils two massive jets pump around 180 tons (176 tonnes) of water every minute—as much as 75 fire engines pumping constantly. This makes them faster and more reliable than hydrofoil ferries.

High-speed catamarans

Hydrofoils and jetfoils are not the only types of high-speed ferries. Catamarans are boats with two separate hulls side by side. Their narrow hulls sit higher in the water and so create less drag or water resistance. Waves do not slow them down because

In light seas hydrofoils are quite stable. They cut through small waves easily.

When the waves are big, hydrofoils ride up and down them. This is called pitching.

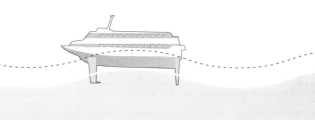

Medium-sized waves move the hydrofoil up and down but do not make it pitch a lot.

they can travel underneath the boat without crashing into the two hulls.

Large catamarans used as ferries can travel at speeds of around 46 mph (74km/h). In 1990 a 100-ft (30-m) catamaran called *Hoverspeed Great Britain*, which was used as a ferry between England and France, crossed the Atlantic Ocean in a record-breaking time of three and a half days.

This ferry is a trimaran—it has three hulls. Waves travel between them under the boat.

A missile-carrying jetfoil used by the U.S. Navy. These warships have three engines.

Fast military boats

Navies around the world do not have just huge battleships and aircraft carrier ships. They also use many small, high-speed boats. These small boats are often useful because they are very quick and difficult for the enemy to spot.

Military boats may look like ordinary vessels, but they are usually much faster and more manoeuvrable. They are also much stronger than ordinary boats because they need to carry armaments, such as guns and missile launchers and to withstand hits from enemy gunfire. Special materials are used to keep them afloat in dangerous conditions.

Patrol and assault craft

Since 1995 the U.S. Navy has used the Mark V Special Operations Craft as their main high-speed boat. Around 80 ft (24m) long, it has a V-shaped hull and can travel at speeds of up to 58 mph (93km/h). It is designed as a rapid-response boat for sending combat swimmers into trouble zones. It can be launched either from a harbour or lowered by crane from the deck of a warship.

Another popular military powerboat, the 51-foot-long (15-m) Avanti, can travel at high speeds thanks to its 1,000-horsepower engines. Built from fibreglass, the hull has foam-filled cavities to give it extra buoyancy so it will not sink very easily. The Avanti has two crew cabins, a galley (kitchen) and an engine room. The cockpit includes advanced navigation and communication equipment.

Navy hydrofoils

Boeing, which also make aeroplanes and rockets, designed some hydrofoil boats for the U.S. Navy. They built six jetfoil warships for the navies of NATO (North Atlantic Treaty Organization) countries. Each boat had three water-jet engines. Two 800-horsepower diesel engines were used for pushing the hull through the water at slow speeds. The other engine was a 17,000-horsepower gas turbine for making the boat move at high speed. Gas turbine engines are similar to steam turbines.

A high-speed Storm class gunboat used by the Norwegian Navy.

Navigation and safety

Many boats operate out at sea where there are no landmarks, so they have to rely on special devices to find their way around. With well over 12 million pleasure boats in the United States, safety is also a big concern.

Modern boats have electronic equipment that makes navigating much easier and safer. Most ocean-going boats have a device called a Global Positioning System (GPS). It is like a small electronic compass that bounces signals off a satellite high up in space. The signals that come back from the satellite tell the boat precisely where it is on Earth to within a few feet. Radar helps high-speed boats navigate in poor weather, when they

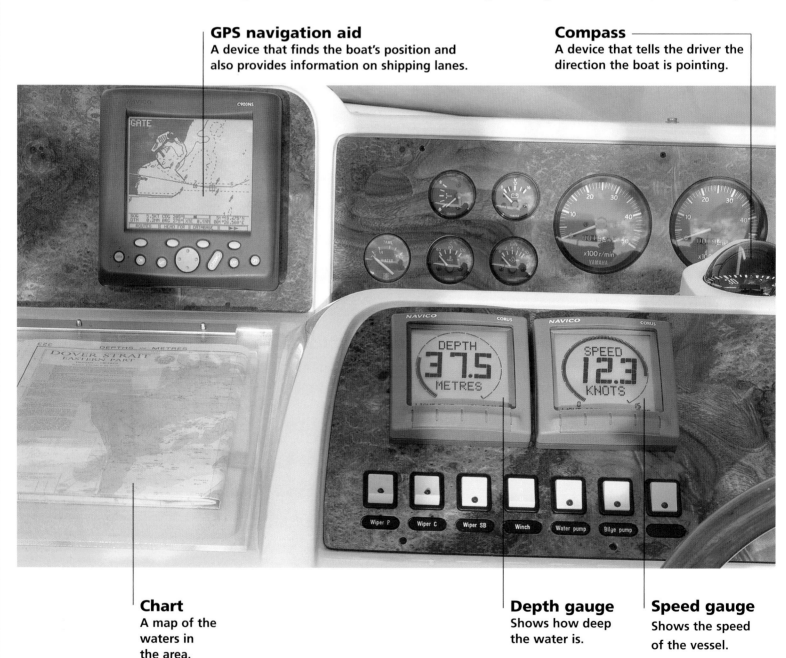

GPS navigation aid
A device that finds the boat's position and also provides information on shipping lanes.

Compass
A device that tells the driver the direction the boat is pointing.

Chart
A map of the waters in the area.

Depth gauge
Shows how deep the water is.

Speed gauge
Shows the speed of the vessel.

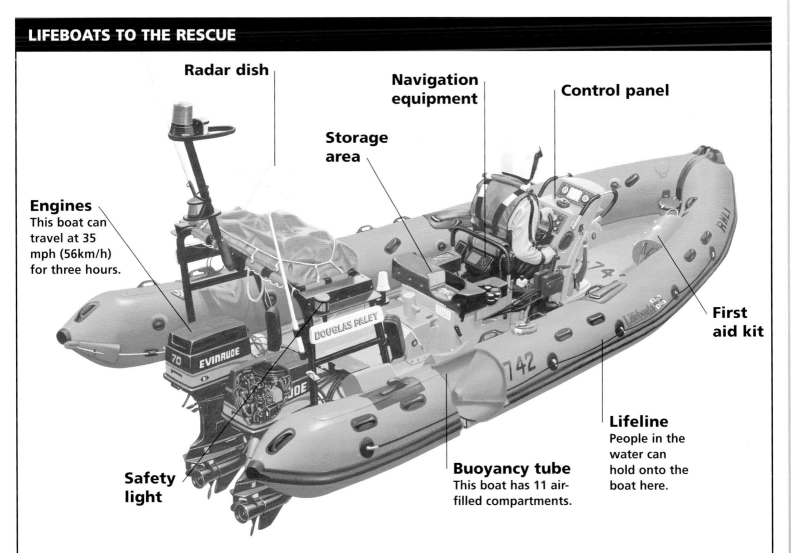

Radar dish

Navigation equipment

Control panel

Storage area

Engines
This boat can travel at 35 mph (56km/h) for three hours.

First aid kit

Safety light

Buoyancy tube
This boat has 11 air-filled compartments.

Lifeline
People in the water can hold onto the boat here.

When boats get into difficulties, air-sea rescue helicopters and lifeboats are on hand to help out. Lifeboats are tough powerboats that will not sink even in the roughest seas. They range in size from small inflatable boats that can carry only five or six people to large ocean-going boats that can carry the crews of large ships. Even if they capsize (turn over), many lifeboats can right themselves in a few minutes using special water tanks or inflatable bags. They are packed with lots of lifesaving equipment, including rockets to fire safety lines to stranded ships, climbing nets to help people aboard, stretchers and medical equipment.

cannot see where they are going. The boat sends out a beam of radio waves and the way this beam is reflected back shows where other boats are and how fast they are moving.

Taking care

All boat users must follow sets of rules called the International Rules (for ocean waters) and the Inland Rules (for the rivers, canals and lakes within the United States). They explain what boats should do when they meet one another and what sort of navigation lights they need. The four main ones are two white lights on top of the mast and at the stern (rear) of the boat, a red light on the left (port) side and a green light on the right (starboard) side. A boat's horn is also used to communicate with other boat crews.

Being safe also means taking precautions, such as being careful that petrol fumes do not build up in the bottom of the boat and keeping life jackets and rafts on board.

Formula One racers

Formula One powerboats can easily reach speeds of 120 mph (200km/h). Although they are very exciting to race, they can also be very dangerous. For this reason all F1 boats are equipped with special safety devices.

A typical Formula One (F1) boat looks quite like an aeroplane without wings. The driver sits behind a sharp pointed nose in a small cockpit that contains a steering wheel, pedals and various instruments mounted on a dashboard. The driver's cockpit sits on a pair of fibreglass hulls called a catamaran. At the front of the boat the hulls taper into two sharp points called

pickleforks that slice through the water. Power comes from a very big half-gallon (2-l) outboard motor. The whole boat is about 20 ft (6m) long and 8 ft (2.5m) wide.

Designed for safety

With F1 boats racing at high speeds near other fast powerboats, safety is extremely important. Both the pickleforks and the nose section are designed to crumple in a crash. This makes the boat slow down gradually and keeps the driver from being crushed in the crash. An F1 boat can travel fast because of its sleek, aeroplane-like design; but if it

Formula One racing boats zoom off at the start of an exciting high-speed race.

High-speed crashes are common during F1 races. The boats are designed to protect the driver.

tips beyond a certain angle, the weight of the engine at the back will then make it quickly flip over completely onto its roof. That is how most crashes happen in F1 races.

If the boat does tip over, a huge airbag (like the ones in the front seats of a car) inflates just behind the driver's head. At the same time, water is taken into a special tank at the back of the boat. The water pulls the boat down at the back, while the airbag pushes the cockpit up at the front. The boat soon points straight up like a rocket and that makes it much easier to rescue the driver.

Right: The bow of a crashed boat sticks out of the water. It helps the driver escape.

The uses of powerboats

High-speed boats have many different uses, from police boats and coast-guard work to pleasure cruising and powerboat racing. Many different organizations need boats that are fast, rugged and safe to handle even in the roughest seas and harshest weather.

The U.S. Coast Guard uses boats for rescuing passengers from other boats in trouble out at sea and to make sure people follow the navigation rules and do not speed. Coast guards have also been very active in preventing drug smuggling, particularly in coastal areas such as Florida. The Boston Whaler Justice Class is a typical Coast Guard boat. It has a wide, open deck and the crew can see in all directions. These boats have unsinkable fibreglass hulls that can carry

A water taxi in Venice, Italy. In this city of canals boats are more common than cars.

12 people. The powerful outboard motor can reach speeds of over 50 mph (80km/h).

One boat, many uses
Some high-speed boats are designed to be used in many different ways. A good example is the Swedish-built Storebro. The Swedish Coastal Artillery use it for moving troops and

A powerboat pulls a parasailor. This is a very popular sport at holiday resorts.

also as a naval ambulance. The Chinese customs service equip it with instruments to help them search vessels and detain suspected smugglers. The Swedish Police and Coast Guard use still different versions of the boat. In each case the same fast and highly manoeuvrable boat is carefully tailored to make sure it meets its users' needs.

Work and leisure

There are almost as many uses for high-speed boats as there are boats themselves. They range from the hydrofoil ferries that carry people and cars from Seattle to Vancouver in Canada to the inflatable dinghies with powerful outboard motors used by Greenpeace campaigners to disrupt whale

hunting. Many boats are used simply for pleasure and recreation. They range from simple jet-skis and motorboats that pull water-skiers behind them to the sleek Formula One catamarans and the jet-powered boats that break water-speed records.

A water-skier gets ready to be pulled along the surface of the water by a powerboat.

Sailing into the future

Engineers are always trying to find ways to make boats safer, faster and stronger. Tomorrow's boats will be very different from those used today.

The boats of tomorrow will be made from new types of materials and not plastic and aluminium like today. They may have a new kind of engine that uses something called magnetohydrodynamics. It is a way of making electricity by forcing a very hot gas called a plasma between powerful magnets. Smaller boats might use solar panels to make power from sunlight. Other boats could use a new kind of rigid, rotating sail to generate electricity to power their engine.

Is it a boat? Is it a plane?

One of the biggest challenges is to come up with boats that can travel fast through rough seas. One type of boat that can do this uses the Wing In Ground (WIG) effect. This boat is a cross between a hovercraft (a boat that floats on a cushion of air) and an aeroplane because it flies just above the water.

The U.S. Navy's Sea Shadow is a stealth boat. This means it cannot be seen by normal radar equipment.

SWATH and stealth

Another advanced design is called Small Waterplane Area Twin Hull (SWATH). If you draw a line around the hull of a boat where it meets the water, it shows what is called the waterplane. By making the waterplane as small as possible, engineers have found they can make boats much more steady, even at high speeds. Most SWATH boats are a type of catamaran, but instead of floating, the boat's two hulls sink completely under the water. So the boat looks a bit like a floating oil platform, with the deck above the water and the legs disappearing beneath it.

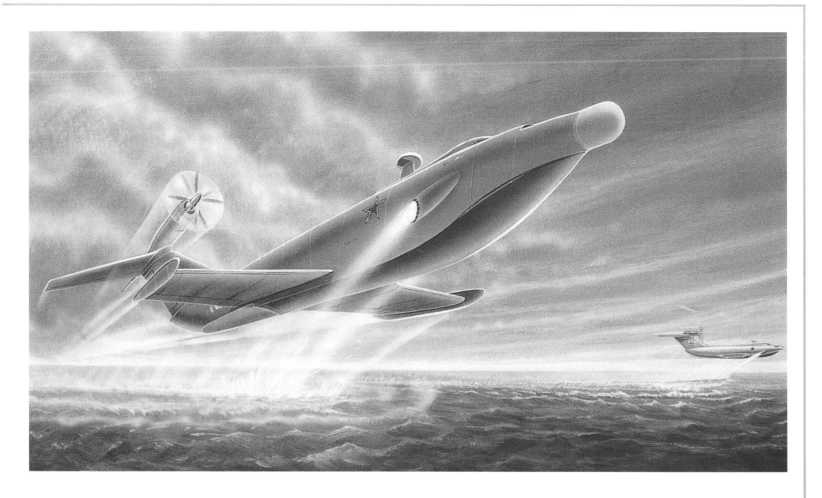

Above: WIG boats, like this one, may one day be a common type of powerboat.

Above: This strange looking boat has a SWATH hull under the water. That keeps it very steady, and so the helicopter can land on it easily.

The U.S. Navy's Sea Shadow is a SWATH boat. It looks like a Stealth bomber aeroplane floating on a SWATH hull. Just like the Stealth bomber, the 150-foot-long (50-m) Sea Shadow is invisible to radar, so it can go on secret missions without being spotted.

FACT FILE

○ One day super-fast ferries with SWATH hulls could be taking people and their cars across oceans in about a day. Cargo vessels could also make deliveries very quickly.

○ Powerboats will never travel as fast as aeroplanes. That is because water is 800 times denser (thicker) than air. Drag forces are therefore much bigger in water.

○ Why not design a new high-speed boat for a special job or sport. What sort of engine would be best: an outboard motor, an inboard engine, or a water jet? Draw pictures of your new boat from different angles and do not forget to design the layout of the cockpit.

Glossary

AIRBAG—a very strong bag that fills up with gas to cushion people during a crash.

BERTH—a bed or bunk on board a boat.

BUOYANCY—the force of water pushing up on a floating object.

BOW—the front end of a boat.

CATAMARAN—a boat with two or more small hulls rather than one.

CAPSIZE—when a boat rolls upside down in the water.

DRAG—a force that pushes against an object when it is moving through air or water.

ENGINE CYLINDER—a part of an engine in which a piston moves up and down to power wheels or propellers.

EXHAUST—the waste gases released from an engines after the fuel has been burned.

FIBREGLASS—a type of plastic made up of many tiny threads of a glasslike substance.

HORSEPOWER—an amount of power that is roughly equal to that of a horse.

HOVERCRAFT—an air-cushion

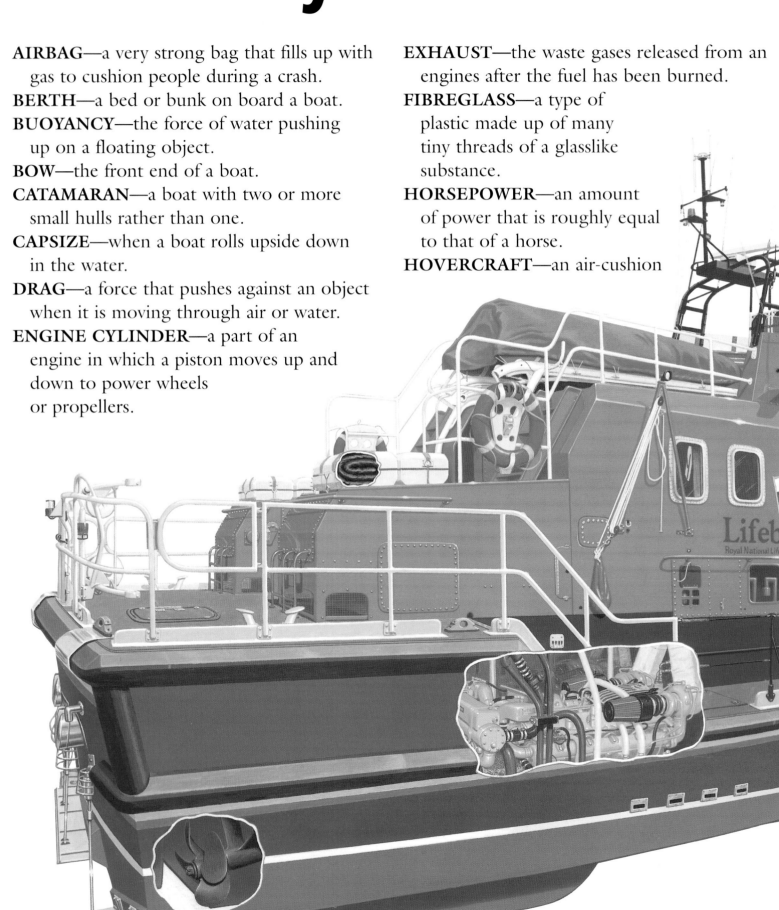

effect vehicle that can cross water and flat stretches of land.

HYDRAULICS—a system that uses pumped liquids to move heavy objects.

JETFOIL—a type of hydrofoil that is pushed along by jets of water.

LANDMARK—a feature of the landscape, such as a hill or river, or a building that helps people find out where they are.

PERSONAL WATERCRAFT—a small leisure craft often powered by a jet drive.

POLYSTYRENE—a very light plastic filled with air bubbles. This plastic floats very well and can be pumped into spaces when hot.

PORT—the left side of a boat.

PRESSURE—the amount of force acting on a particular area of a surface.

FURTHER INFORMATION

Books to read:
Boats (Built for Speed) by Ian Graham.
Raintree Steck-Vaughn; Austin, TX, 1999.
High-Speed Boats by Simon Bornhoft.
Lerner Publications; Minneapolis, MN, 1999.

Web sites to look at:
http://www.powerboatmag.com
http://www.wellcraft.com
http://www.seadoo.com

Alternatively, visit a boat show in your area.

This large lifeboat is a very tough boat used to rescue sailors out at sea far from the shore.

PROPELLER—a metal disk with blades that spins around to push a boat through water.

SPEEDOMETER—an instrument that displays how fast you are travelling.

STARBOARD—the right side of a boat.

STEALTH—a type of technology that makes a plane, truck, or boat invisible to radar.

STERN—the back end of a boat.

STRANDED—when a boat becomes stuck on the seabed in shallow water or on rocks just under the surface.

TRIREME—a boat used by the ancient Greeks. It had 170 rowers in three rows.

TURBINE—a drum covered in propeller-like blades that spins when gases flow past it.

Index